HOW TO TRANSFORM YOUR HOME INTO A CHRISTMAS WONDERLAND

Turn Your Home into Santa's Magical Wonderland!

NORA GREY

How to Transform Your Home into a Christmas Wonderland : Turn Your Home into Santa's Magical Wonderland

NORA GREY

Published by BILLY GRANT, 2024.

HOW TO TRANSFORM YOUR HOME INTO A CHRISTMAS WONDERLAND : TURN YOUR HOME INTO SANTA'S MAGICAL WONDERLAND

First edition. September 17, 2024.

Copyright © 2024 NORA GREY.

ISBN: 979-8227081605

Written by NORA GREY.

Also by NORA GREY

Table of Contents

*To **Edrina Kaareh**, the love that lights up my world like Christmas lights on a cold winter's night, this book is dedicated to you.*

INTRODUCTION

CHRISTMAS HAS A CERTAIN way of transforming even the most basic houses into warm, inviting havens of happiness. And what if you could have more than simply a comfortable home? What if your living room was filled with all the wonder and enchantment of Santa's world this year, with every nook and cranny beaming with joy and every tiny detail reflecting your own unique holiday spirit?

Imagine entering and being instantly carried away to a wintry paradise, where every ornament tells a tale and the sparkling lights outside rival the brilliance of the stars. That's precisely what we're going to do: turn your house into an enchanted Christmas wonderland that seems as though Santa himself decorated it.

The best part is that you can accomplish this without having a degree in interior design or a large bank account. Put an end to pricey department store decorations that make your pocketbook feel less joyful.

We're talking about the allure of do-it-yourself projects, where commonplace materials like paper, twine, and pine cones are turned into creative tools that let you turn your house into a joyful haven that exudes cosiness, originality, and warmth. This is the time of year to really let your hair down, to combine elegance and simplicity, craft and charm, and to keep things enjoyable and uniquely you.

Handmade ornaments are where the magic begins. These, however, are not your average, forgettable store-bought trinkets.

No, these are imaginative fragments that you've proudly displayed on your tree, glowing with the love and effort you put into creating them. Imagine basic paper forms that are joined by a small piece of string and coated with a thin layer of paint. It seems so simple, perhaps too simple, isn't it? That is the key. Its potency comes from its simplicity. What's the best thing, then? These tiny works of art aren't exclusive to your tree. They can be used as adorable gift tags or to hang over mantles or dangle from doorways.

Your hands have suddenly given every nook and cranny of your house that extra dash of Christmas charm.

Next, we go beyond the conventional tree decorating and incorporate something a bit more elaborate: colourful wreaths. a wreath that draws attention rather than merely sitting on your door. We're talking ribbons that lend the ideal touch of festive flair, artificial berries that burst with the vivid colours of winter, and grapevine branches that twist and twirl into an intricate circle.

IT'S SIMILAR TO CREATING a work of live art, in which each component you select has a unique tale to tell. And this wreath becomes more than just decoration once it's hung up. It's a way to say "Welcome to Christmas" to everyone who comes through your door, giving them a warm welcome.

Let's now discuss the dining table, which is the centre of any holiday. You you aware of how everything seems to be drawn to that table? A couple of glasses of eggnog, stories, and laughter. It serves as more than just a restaurant—it's a location to create memories.

And what more exquisite approach to create a focal point for those moments than with an exquisite homemade centrepiece? We're talking about candles that flicker and have a cosy, mellow glow. Pine cones, arranged carelessly to provide a rustic, wintry feel. And for a final touch of enchantment, artificial snow scattered about like a fantasy of the first snowfall. It's not about perfection here. Capturing the natural beauty of nature while allowing the focal point to speak for itself is the goal.

You've made a setting where every meal feels celebratory when the lights go down and the candles flicker.

We must go beyond the interior of your house, though, as the outside offers a first look at the wonderland you've built. Step inside the spectacular outdoor light show. Nothing compares to the enchantment of sparkling lights against a crisp, dark winter night. It resembles preparing for Santa's big arrival. Here's where the fun starts, though: these lights convey stories in addition to being decorations.

They add vitality to your house whether they are hung over bushes, wrapped around trees, or strung along fences. They draw attention to the tiny things, which give the night dimension and transform your front garden into a stage on which the stars above seem to be a part of the action. But first, safety. Because the joy your lights bring should be the only thing brighter than your lights, always use outdoor-rated lights and abide by the manufacturer's instructions.

FURTHERMORE, IT GOES beyond simply hanging lights and calling it a day. Oh no, the extras are where the enjoyment is. Luminous orbs nestled into the snow, lighted garlands winding up the porch railing, and perhaps even a few LED shapes adding just the right touch of whimsical charm. This is where you can really express your creativity. You get to set up a scenario that not only brightens the evening but also entices others to experience the cosiness of your holiday mood. Who knows? People may slow down to take in the magic of your display, making it the talk of the neighbourhood.

Everything you need, including paper, rope, candles, and pine cones, is in front of you. The true essence of Christmas magic lies not in department store price tags but rather in the creator's heart and hands. You. With each DIY project, you're not simply adding décor to your home, you're weaving your character into every nook, every light, and every sparkle.

CHAPTER 1
HANDMADE CHRISTMAS ORNAMENTS

Making your own decorations adds a certain something that no ornament from the store can match. You have the power to transform ordinary materials into something spirited and unique that expresses your identity and the holiday you wish to create. Personalised ornaments are more than just decorations; they're fragments of you dispersed among the branches, each one revealing a different tale at every turn of the eye. With its memories and unique touches, your tree starts to take on the sense of an old friend that could never be replicated by cheap tinsel.

Starting with anything as basic as paper is an option. A few sheets—possibly ones that have been laying around unutilized—transform into something else all of a sudden. A few folds and cuts can create hearts, stars, or snowflakes. Your ornament can still be attractive without being elaborate; its charm comes from its slightly off-center cut and rough edges. It starts to add to the allure.

When you hang these up, you'll see how the lights catch them and create dancing shadows across the space. Just like the snowflakes that fall outside your window, each one is distinct and no two are same.

Consider what you already have in your home, such as buttons, worn-out ribbons, and extra fabric scraps. They are merely there, ready to be transformed into a joyous occasion. With a little glue and perseverance, these abandoned objects can now be brought to life with festive charm.

Those buttons? They turn into focus on a charming little snowman. That bow? It nestles cosy among the branches and encircles a small gift box you've made. Each piece is a narrative that you have skilfully put together.

Pine cones are yet another creative gold mine. They give your Christmas tree a rustic, earthy feel and are free, fresh from nature. Take a few from outdoors, give them a quick cleaning, and then let your creativity run wild. A dab of white paint to simulate the look of frost or a sprinkling of glitter to perfectly capture candlelight will make a big difference. With a little twine or string wrapped around the top, you can easily create an ornament that would look great in a cabin during the winter.

But simplicity isn't everything. You want to take risks and be bolder sometimes. Why not make some eye-catching ornaments? For this, Clay is ideal. All you need is some air-dry clay, a rolling pin, and cookie cutters; no kiln or sophisticated equipment is required. Press your shapes into it, roll it out, and allow it to dry.

Before you know it, you'll have strong, lovely pieces that can be simple for a more natural look, painted, or glittering. You can hang anything you like, stars, reindeer, Christmas trees—you can make them all shine brightly from the limbs of your tree.

What about felt, then? A craftsperson's best friend, felt is soft, colourful, and simple to work with. You cut out forms, such as a small gingerbread man or a Christmas stocking, fill them with some cotton to make them feel plump and cosy, and sew them together with thread.

It's a handmade item that adds cosiness to your tree; just tie a ribbon around the top. Every stitch brings a small piece of you into the holiday season, making it meaningful and personal.

Beads are great for people who enjoy a little shine in their life. You may make decorations for your tree that sparkle like little stars. Take some wire, string on a variety of vibrant beads, and then twist and bend it into any shape you choose, such as stars, snowflakes, or even abstract forms that give your decor a contemporary edge.

When the light hits them at precisely the correct angle, colour glints will bounce about the space. And it's quite simple! Anyone can link beads together, even if they're not very crafty, and the end effect will make you feel as like you've just perfected the art of Christmas magic.

The way these handcrafted ornaments all come together is what makes them so beautiful. One by one, they add unique touches to your tree—moments from your life sewn, adhered, or twisted into shape. They are unique because they aren't flawless.

It's intentional that your tree won't appear as though it was taken straight out of a department store window. It's infused with your personality and the vacation you've planned for your loved ones.

Imagine for a moment that tree, softly shining in the twilight light. Perhaps there's a crackling fire nearby, and the room is filled with the aroma of pine. Every ornament has a backstory, be it a memory from this year or previous years, a friend's present, or something you crafted one lazy afternoon.

These are more than just decorations; they're mementos that will bring back memories every time you take them out of the box the following year. and the subsequent year. They are more than just ornaments for your tree; they are an integral element of the custom and the occasion.

And that is the whole magic of it. A store may sell you a tree full of shiny, well-made decorations, but nothing will ever have the same sentimental value as something you produced yourself.

Making your own ornaments is a great way to preserve memories and create something that will last much longer than any box of commercially purchased ornaments. By bringing a part of yourself into the holidays and hanging it for everyone to see, you're doing more than just decorating.

In a day when anything can be purchased with a single click, there's something unique about taking your time and creating something by hand. It gives the holiday a feeling of community and cosiness that is unmatched by anything prepackaged.

Your home is filled with that unmistakable Christmas magic via the process of creation, whether it's a simple paper snowflake or an elaborate beaded ornament.

Crafting Paper Ornaments with Everyday Materials

Let your creativity run wild with some scissors, an assortment of outdated magazines, and possibly any leftover gift wrap remnants you salvaged from last year. Something about turning regular paper into magical Christmas decorations makes me happy. It's like piece by piece transforming the ordinary into the extraordinary. A few folds and cuts are all that are needed to create a paper star. You can begin by cutting out tiny hearts and stars and experimenting with different forms that appeal to you. Perhaps the traditional design of a Christmas tree or a hanging bell sets the mood. You already have the supplies you need in your house; they're just hiding in plain sight, waiting to be transformed into a festive creation.

Flatten out that cereal box you were going to throw away. You may quickly use that drab brown surface as the basis for your festive paper ornaments. Cut out a few shapes, such as stars, trees, or if you're very daring, a snowflake.

Get those markers, leftover spray paint, or even nail polish if you're feeling extra daring and add some colour. Add vivid colours, patterns, and motifs on those lifeless surfaces to make your ornaments stand out. The finest aspect? Everybody is unique. A little crimson here, a little glitter there, and all of a sudden your house feels warm and full of bits and pieces of you.

It's not necessary to be an expert craftsperson to do something exceptional. Engage the whole family and let the children design their own unique shapes.

It's possible to come out looking more like a blob than a bell, but that's part of the appeal. The attraction is in imperfections; the small details in the design accentuate the handmade feel. Perhaps you want to go simple and maintain a minimalistic style by using only white paper. Alternatively, you could like a vibrant burst of colour that energises your tree. It's all up to you, any way.

Consider adding some texture to those paper stars if you're feeling very creative.

BEFORE UNFOLDING, GIVE them a slightly crumpled appearance to give the impression that they have been hanging at the North Pole for a long time. Adding a layer of glitter to create a frosted effect will transform your ordinary paper star into an heirloom from out of Santa's workshop. Don't stop there. Take out those old buttons from your sewing kit and use glue to attach them as tiny decorations to the paper ornaments. Who would have thought that an old button with a missing pair might be revived and used as a festive addition to your tree?

There are countless ideas when it comes to paper crafts. You may quickly make a garland by stringing many paper circles together. One loop at a time, let the colours change to red, green, and gold, and see how your room begins to feel festive. Alternatively, attempt something more complex. When you peel the paper apart, you'll get a row of interconnected stars or Christmas trees. Fold the paper into accordion pleats and cut shapes out of the folds. The sense of accomplishment one has while using such basic resources to create something so striking? It is unbeatable.

Also, don't confine yourself to simple forms. With a few small cuts here and there, paper cones can simply be transformed into Christmas trees. You may create a whimsical forest in your living room by stacking, painting, and adding small pom-poms on the top. It doesn't need to be difficult. A little paper inventiveness goes a long way.

Look through your cupboard for supplies; brown paper bags work well as homemade ornament canvases. Cut them into strips, fold them into star patterns, or twist and braid them into wreath forms.

The warm, homely vibe of brown paper can enhance the cosiness of your Christmas décor. For an organic, handcrafted charm, adorn them with twine, dried fruit, or even sprigs of greenery.

It's the unexpected that has the magic. Perhaps there was another use for those old doilies that were gathering dust in the drawer. After folding them into the shapes of snowflakes, hang them from the windows and see how the light catches them, creating beautiful shadows that dance across the space. That ancient map you've stashed away in the closet's back?

Cut it into star shapes, allowing the roads and lines to give each ornament a distinct visual texture. You may also use newspaper to create rustic ornaments with an antique feel. Immediately transform an old piece into something completely new by applying some gold paint to the edges.

Additionally, remember to use paper for your present tags. Make tiny squares out of the leftover parts from your ornaments. Your presents can now be completely customised by adding a little string. Your packages will have a handmade touch that unites everything, in place of the generic store-bought tags.

Making things seem nice isn't the only thing that goes into paper crafting. The key is to take what you already have and turn it into something meaningful. Seeing bits of paper that were previously hidden in your house come to life and add colour to your tree fills you with a unique sense of happiness. It's also about the creative process rather than just the final output. That's the time when you get down with a bunch of scissors, glue, and paper scraps and allow your hands transform something commonplace into something spectacular.

Paper has this way of making everything feel more personal. It's light-hearted, light-hearted, and malleable. It can be made elegant or basic. You can paint, fold, twist, or shred it. The options are unlimited. You are creating memories with each piece, not simply ornaments, that will hang on your tree this year and every year after that, gaining significance with each passing holiday season.

Adding String and Decorative Flair

More than just a simple form will do to make your ornaments truly stand out; you also need to add that unique touch that makes them uniquely yours. The string, a little but powerful feature that does more than just hang the ornament on the tree, is where it all begins. You may use a piece of ribbon you've recycled from an old gift, thin twine, or colourful thread.

Taking great care to thread your ornaments and make sure they hang at the ideal height will give your Christmas tree the ultimate harmony. Every component seems to have been thoughtfully arranged by elves as it sways gently and perfectly catches the light.

But when you can go farther, why stop at string? Where the true fun starts is when you add that extra flair. Imagine a swath of glitter scattered over your decorations, glistening under the Christmas lights. Perhaps it's not just glitter; perhaps each piece has small painted snowflakes or golden stars that are meticulously hand-drawn to provide even more appeal. Those little things are what really count. Every ornament ought to feel as though the festive spirit has kissed it; each one should resemble a tiny bit of enchantment hanging from the branches.

THREADING THE DECORATIONS is becoming a craft unto itself. The string should enhance rather than overshadow the design. The secret is to keep the string understated so that the ornament takes centre stage. A tiny thread of gold or silver, or even clear fishing line, will draw attention to the focal point of the piece. For a more whimsical touch, consider using red-and-white baker's twine to evoke sentiments of bygone Christmas seasons. You're creating an environment and making every move matter—you're not simply hanging decorations.

AFTER THE STRING HAS been strung, you should consider where you want the ornament to go. It all comes down to spacing. Your tree will appear cluttered if it is too close together; sparse if it is too far away. It has a certain rhythm and equilibrium. The decorations should appear to be floating in space and slowly swirling in response to air movement. While some should be positioned further up the tree, where the lights can create striking shadows, others should hang low, towards the tips of the branches.

FOR A MINUTE, LET'S talk about glitter. It's one of those items that has the ability to suddenly change an ordinary object into something spectacular. A little goes a long way, so you don't need to cover your decorations in it completely. The sculpture has a frosted appearance that is achieved by lightly brushing glue onto the edges and then dusting it with fine glitter. The subtle shimmer is what attracts the eye and highlights the small features. The trick is to apply it just right—not too thickly nor too sparingly.

It's important to know when to quit, just like with the best decorations.

Of course, there are other ways to add flair than glitter. Consider arranging textures in layers. Perhaps you attach a little button to the middle of a star or wrap a tiny ribbon around the bottom of a hanging decoration. The compositions feel more deliberate and meaningful because of these small details. You could also paint on some designs, like little holly leaves towards the top or a candy cane stripe around the edge.

The ornament feels like more than simply another decoration because of these nuances, which give it character and depth.

Witnessing an ornament come to life with a few strategically placed details is very fulfilling. Your design gains a subtle dimension when you incorporate small beads or sequins into it. It's not necessary to go overboard; a little bead on the edge of a paper star or a few sequins scattered around a tree form can have a big impact. The small details are what give the complete ensemble a lift and give your tree a unique shine.

Additionally, you can experiment with unconventional materials. Consider tying a string of tiny bells around it so that the ornament gently jingles as it travels. You may also add some pinecones to the top to give it a rustic, natural look. Use any extra wrapping paper to create miniature forms that you can use as decoration. You can overlay patterns, experiment with colour, and add intrigue to the design. The idea is to enjoy yourself and let your originality shine through in each ornament.

Not to be overlooked is colour. The appropriate colour scheme may bring everything together and give your tree a unified appearance. You may choose a theme, such as classic reds, green, and gold, or go more contemporary with blues, silvers, and whites. As you embellish, consider how each component complements the others. Does the way the glitter reflects the light improve the overall appearance? Does the string draw attention to itself without detracting from the colours?

It all comes down to harmonising and allowing each element to shine in its unique way.

There's no haste when working on these ornaments. Allow each to develop as you proceed. It may begin as just a plain star, but as soon as you add the thread, the glitter, and the small painted embellishments, it becomes something entirely original. Both literally and conceptually, the thread pulls everything together, directing the design while highlighting your unique touches.

CHAPTER 2
THE PERFECT WREATH – WELCOMING GUESTS IN STYLE

A wreath serves as an invitation as much as a decoration. It's the first thing people see when they arrive at your door; it's a warm welcome to your home from the moment someone knocks. More than just colour or symmetry, the goal of crafting the ideal wreath is to condense the spirit of the season into a single, jolly circle. Your wreath sets the tone for what's behind that door, whether you like to keep things classic or go crazy with unusual details. It alludes to the delights that lie within, bringing with it warmth, humour, and the distinct charm of the season.

Commence with the base. The feel of evergreen branches in your hands as you weave them into that traditional spherical form has a certain gratifying quality. Whether they are real or fake, they serve as the foundation and the framework that keeps your idea coherent. Not only are you shaping a space with each turn and tuck, but you're also creating a welcoming atmosphere that nearly cries out for hot chocolate and Christmas carols by the fireplace. If you go for the real thing, the aroma of pine fills the air with that distinct whiff of winter and brings back memories of joyous nights and snow-covered trees. It's mood, not just adornment.

Let's now incorporate some personality. Don't accept the typical bows and berries. Consider the layers, the texture, and the ways in which each element might enhance the narrative your wreath attempts to convey.

Perhaps it's the rich, spicy aroma emanating from bundles of cinnamon sticks bound together with thread. Alternatively, you might go for dried oranges, since their vivid hue and delicate aroma pay homage to vintage holiday customs. Not only are you making a wreath, but you're also combining textures and smells to create a sensory overload that greets guests as soon as they arrive on your porch.

A certain amount of artistry is necessary, but it need not be flawless. There are moments when the turmoil has beauty.

You could add eucalyptus or rosemary sprigs that poke out at random angles, or you could leave a few strands of ivy trailing wildly from the bottom to give the illusion that the wreath is growing as it hangs. It is not required to be exact. It must have life, as though it has just been taken from a wintry garden, dusted with frost, and placed triumphantly on your front door. It's the flaws, like the slightly crooked berries or the ribbon that wildly coils in the wind, that make it unforgettable.

AND SPEAKING OF RIBBONS, this is the really exciting part. Disregard the typical pre-made bows that you can purchase from any craft store. It must pop for you to want it to. Perhaps it's a deep crimson velvet ribbon, or perhaps it's a plaid design that takes you back to warm flannel sweaters and cold nights spent by the hearth. Why not use lace instead? Something unexpected and elegant that made a gentle contrast with the rugged foliage. Layering is key; let one ribbon flow in loose loops and catch the light as it moves, or let one ribbon weave among the branches. The goal is to make it seem simple, even if you took 30 minutes to perfect it.

Don't be afraid to incorporate features into your wreath design that may seem out of the ordinary. While pinecones are a traditional addition, how about tiny wooden snowflakes? Or perhaps a series of small bells that gently tinkle each time the door opens? You may also use bits of fabric, such swatches from holiday blankets that have sentimental value or vintage scarves. These minute embellishments give your wreath personality and elevate it above a basic holiday decoration to something incredibly unique.

The fascinating part comes in the colour scheme. Though they are always dependable, traditional red and green are not required. Gold and silver add a hint of refinement and perfectly capture the winter light. Perhaps you want to create a frosted effect with white, silver, and blue hues, giving the impression that your wreath was taken directly out of a forest blanketed in snow.

ALTERNATELY, USE WARM earth tones—burnt oranges, rich burgundy, and copper accents that shine against the background of foliage—for a more rustic vibe.

As the wreath begins to take shape, consider the finishing details. A wreath seems incomplete without a little glitter. You could weave tiny fairy lights between the branches; they would be modest enough to glimmer without drawing attention away from the foliage's inherent beauty. Alternatively, you may choose for delicate embellishments hidden among the foliage, like tiny glass balls or interestingly shaped wooden creatures. They will draw attention without taking centre stage.

The traditional location for a door is in the middle, but why not get a little creative? For a more rustic look, try hanging it from a thick rope; alternatively, go asymmetrical and place it slightly to the side for a contemporary twist. To really bring home that warm, festive feeling, you could even incorporate it into a larger display by putting lanterns on either side or framing your door with garlands.

It's important to consider your wreath as the focal point of your outdoor holiday décor; it should take centre stage without being overpowering.

And the most enjoyable aspect about creating your own wreath? It becomes a reflection of you, your home, and what you want to express to the world over the holidays. It's not about perfection. It's all about combining the colours, textures, and scents that appeal to you.

Perhaps that calls for keeping to classic components like berries and holly, or perhaps it calls for something wholly unconventional, like feathers or old decorations from the tree you grew up with. Regardless of the design you decide on, your wreath serves as a kind of signal to your guests that they are entering a loving, joyful, and festive space.

Building the Foundation with Grapevine and Greenery

Grapevine wreaths may appear straightforward at first, but their unprocessed, twisted nature—the way they organically curve and tangle—has a certain elegance. With the base, this is where it all starts. There's no need to hurry. Start by feeling the texture and bend of each piece as you run your fingers down the thick, rustic vines. Whether you gather the vines yourself or purchase them from a craft store, grapevine wreaths have an earthy, organic vibe that sets the tone for the entire arrangement. It is a blank canvas just waiting to be embellished to create something truly festive.

Take hold of that wreath and listen to its desires as you begin to create it. Don't force it into a perfect circle—let the vines loop and overlap naturally, the way nature intended. The allure of grapevine wreaths resides in their slightly untamed, worn-in appearance. You're not making a factory-perfect wreath; rather, you're making something unique and distinctly your own, full of personality and Christmas flair.

Working with grapevine is magical because it's flexible, forgiving, and brimming with possibilities. It's time to add some foliage now.

Embroidery adds life to your wreath. It all comes down to weaving the artificial sprigs into the vines, whether you're using artificial ones or fresh pine branches that you clipped from the backyard. You don't have to be concerned about accuracy. Begin by arranging the pieces in various directions, allowing some to hang loosely and others to fit snugly into the spaces between.

Whichever you choose, as long as it creates that lush, festive vibe, will do—pine, fir, or cedar. The secret is to make it appear natural, as if the wreath spontaneously took on its shape after being bitten by a winter frost. It's more important to create something that feels inviting, alive, and fresh than something that is extremely polished.

Next are the plastic berries. Mixing artificial and natural elements may seem strange at first, but here's where the fun comes in.

Your wreath has a holiday feel without overpowering the senses thanks to the contrast created by the brilliant pops of red against the dark green. Disperse them, tucking them under the foliage so that they protrude like tiny jewels. Like lost treasures just waiting to be discovered, some may gather in one spot while others might scatter themselves throughout the wreath. Like the punctuation marks in your design, berries attract the eye without taking centre stage.

IT ALL COMES DOWN TO balance—but not the kind you have to consider too much. Let the wreath take shape as you go, trusting your instincts. If something feels right, it probably is. And don't be afraid to get creative with other textures, too. Toss in a few sprigs of eucalyptus or rosemary to add dimension and a subtle fragrance. These details elevate your wreath from ordinary to something uniquely yours. The unexpected combination of materials—pine, grapevine, eucalyptus—makes it a little unpredictable, a little wild, and that's exactly the point. You're not just decorating; you're crafting a piece of the holiday season that feels organic and lived-in.

Once the greenery is in place, step back for a moment. The wreath should feel full, but not overstuffed. The grapevine should still peek through in places, offering glimpses of its raw, natural form. This is the foundation—strong, simple, and ready for whatever festive touches you decide to add next.

As you hold that base in your hands, there's a certain satisfaction in knowing that you're working with something so elemental.

The grapevine, twisted and bent into shape, becomes the heart of your design. It's sturdy, but not rigid, allowing you to weave and layer freely. The greenery draped across it softens the edges, making the whole thing feel alive, as though it's reaching out to welcome the winter chill. But the wreath isn't done yet. There's more to build, more to bring into this circle of holiday spirit.

Think about the little details. A few pinecones nestled into the corners, their woody texture adding a rustic charm.

Tuck them into the branches, as if they've naturally fallen there, caught in the vines as they grew. Or maybe you prefer something more delicate, like a few strands of dried flowers or tiny bundles of cinnamon sticks tied with twine. These details aren't just decorative; they're pieces of memory, bringing the scents and textures of the season into focus. Each element you add builds on the story the wreath tells, layer by layer.

It's in these small touches where your personality shines through. Maybe you go for a more minimal look, letting the grapevine and greenery do most of the talking, or maybe you pile on the decor, filling the wreath with baubles and trinkets until it almost overflows with holiday cheer. The point is, there's no right or wrong way to build it. Just as every home has its own traditions, every wreath takes on a life of its own, shaped by the hands that create it.

If you're feeling adventurous, try threading in some ribbon. A thick, bold ribbon in a festive red or gold can transform your wreath from simple to spectacular.

WRAP IT LOOSELY AROUND the wreath, letting it weave in and out of the branches like a ribbon winding through a gift. Or maybe you prefer something more subtle, a thin piece of twine or a ribbon in muted tones that complements the natural colors of the greenery. The way the ribbon curls and flows adds movement, making the wreath feel dynamic, alive with the spirit of the season.

And then, there's the option to add a little sparkle. Maybe it's a string of fairy lights twinkling through the branches, casting a soft glow that catches the eye as it flickers in the evening light. Or perhaps it's a dusting of glitter, applied sparingly to the tips of the greenery so that it sparkles just enough to feel magical, without overpowering the natural beauty of the wreath. The lights, the glitter, these finishing touches create that final layer of holiday wonder, bringing your wreath to life in the most festive way possible.

Ribbons and Creative Customizations

Grab the ribbon, and don't overthink it—this is where your wreath really takes on that extra spark. Ribbons have a way of transforming the most basic wreath into something special, like the final flourish on a wrapped gift. Start by picking the right colors—maybe the deep reds and greens of a classic Christmas, or go bold with metallic golds and silvers for a touch of glamour. The textures matter too. Satin for a smooth, rich look or burlap if you're leaning toward rustic charm. These little choices will shape the whole vibe of your wreath.

Now comes the fun part—bow-making. It's not as tricky as it sounds. You want your bow to feel full and festive, not stiff or forced. Start by looping the ribbon loosely in your hand, creating soft folds. Pinch the center and secure it with a piece of floral wire or string, letting the loops puff out naturally. Don't worry about symmetry. Let it be slightly uneven, with the tails trailing off in different lengths. That imperfect, handmade look adds charm and character.

The bow should feel almost effortless, like it was designed to fall into position on your wreath.

Once your bow is ready, it's all about placing. Tuck it in snugly at the base, off-center, or directly at the top. Wherever you lay it, the ribbon should flow like a natural extension of the wreath. Let the tails hang down, curling and twisting through the greenery, as if they're dancing in the cold wind. You can even let them drape off the bottom of the wreath, providing a sense of movement.

If your wreath feels a little too stiff, the ribbon will soften it up fast.

But don't stop at just one ribbon. Layer different widths, textures, and colors. Start with a thicker, more solid ribbon as your base, then weave in a narrower ribbon with a contrasting texture or color. Maybe even add a sheer or lace ribbon for that delicate touch. The layers of ribbon will provide depth and make the wreath feel rich and full, like it's filled with festive cheer. The blend of colourful ribbons offers a fun, dynamic sense that captures the eye and pulls you into the festive attitude.

Now, here's where you can really get creative. Customizing your wreath is what makes it yours, so think beyond just ribbons. Take any leftover shreds of fabric from earlier Christmas crafts and tie them into small bows or knots around the wreath. These unexpected bursts of texture can create a homey, handcrafted atmosphere. Or use strips of plaid fabric, tied loosely in knots to bring in a winter cabin vibe. These are the tiny touches that add a warm, personalised feel to your wreath.

Remember to choose seasonal colours. Although red and green are the traditional colours, you can experiment with a full range of seasonal tones. To give your wreath a crisp, wintery feel, add some frosty whites or ice blues. Alternatively, use rich, deep purples and golds to give it an opulent, rich tone. Your mantle and tree decorations should blend together to create a unified winter fantasy, with the colours acting as an extension of your house. That spirit of joy should be reflected in every ribbon and scrap of fabric, a small piece of you in every fold.

But let's also discuss texturing. Layering is all about Christmas, both in terms of colour and texture. Add velvet ribbons to the wreath to give it a cosy, inviting atmosphere that entices people to reach out and touch it. For a more rustic, outdoor aesthetic that will remind you of the earthy scents of pine forests, add burlap or twine. Sequins and metallic threads will catch the light and twinkle against the greenery like stars if you're going for a glam look. It's important to combine different textures and allow them to come together organically. This gives the wreath a tiered, luxurious look without making it seem overly finished.

Don't just stick everything on and call it a day when it comes to security. A few berries may be wound through the loops, or a stem of holly could be slipped under the ribbon to give the impression that nature herself has put the finishing touches. This is the point at which your wreath begins to take on life of its own, becoming more than simply a simple assembly that changes and expands with each addition.

It becomes more than just a decoration when you personalise it; it becomes a representation of the enchantment of the season.

You can even embellish the wreath with tiny mementos or trinkets. Perhaps fasten a few small bells or vintage Christmas decorations from previous occasions. These unique touches, tiny mementos of bygone winters, give that warm, nostalgic feeling. Just watch out that they don't overshadow the wreath—they're meant to be accents, not focal points.

CHAPTER 3
TABLE CENTERPIECES – SETTING THE FESTIVE MOOD FOR MEALS

A Christmas supper should feel like its own holiday party, with each gaze across the table representing more than simply the food on the plate. Where the magic starts is at the centrepiece. The goal is to add celebratory touches that make people smile even before they've had a taste. It's not about overdoing the table. Imagine a lavish arrangement of greenery and flickering candles.

The aroma of pine mixed with the gentle brightness that reflected off the plates and glasses. It's straightforward, but it brings everything together in a cosy, welcoming way.

Commence with the base. Collect what you have; don't go overboard. A few pinecones, some fake berries and some evergreen sprigs from the yard. Arrange them so that a bed of winter flora forms the ideal backdrop without drawing attention to itself. Lay them across the table runner. The subtle landscape you're building will let the details—the true magic—shine through. Allow the branches to cascade organically over the table, wavy and curved as though they belonged there and nature had created the setting.

Now for the candles. This is where your warmth is needed. Instead of thinking large and aggressive, consider placing little votive clusters throughout the foliage. The glow is more personal the smaller the candles. Arrange them at various elevations to create a whimsical, glittering look.

LED candles are also a great option if real candles seem too dangerous (since, let's face it, children and pets don't mix well with open flames). The arrangement is key to creating the illusion that light is dancing among the leaves and illuminating the dishes and faces seated around the table with gentle shadows and flashes of light.

You need some texture to contrast with the glow and the greens. This is the time to incorporate metallics, but not too much. Imagine little gold decorations tucked into the foliage, or silver bells strewn among the pinecones.

These delicate sparkling accents draw the attention and provide a festive, opulent touch without being garish. The secret is moderation. Here's a shimmer, there's a shine. You are crafting a moment, not ornamenting a tree.

Speaking of moments, this is the place where one can add a personal touch. Perhaps it's a few cinnamon sticks bound with string, or thoughtfully arranged dried orange slices within the greenery. These tiny details give your guests an immersive experience by adding texture, fragrance, and visual intrigue.

The perfume of cinnamon and citrus instantly transports you to a warm and comfortable place. The goal is to create a space that feels thoughtful, kind, and intimately linked to the season, not about perfection.

Never hesitate to use what you already have. Take out any outdated decorations that aren't fit for the tree and give them a fresh look. Perhaps a set of little miniatures or perhaps an old-fashioned toy evokes fond memories. Allow them to be a part of your centrepiece, a little bit of personality added here and there.

Every element conveys a narrative, and this arrangement ought to do the same—tell the tale of your festive season, your celebrations, and the memories you hope to make around the table.

Consider your centerpiece's height. Nothing too tall or hefty, as you want people to be able to see each other across the table. Maintain a low profile and a wide layout, but make sure there's enough variation to draw the viewer's attention. A glass vase loaded with ornaments or a tiered cake stand decorated with candles and greenery are two examples of items you can elevate. It's about building layers in a way that feels organic—as if everything fell just where it was supposed to. Not in a convoluted way.

Consider the rest of your holiday decor while choosing colours. If your tree is decked out in red and gold, incorporate those hues into your centrepiece by stringing ribbons through the foliage or scattering tiny red berries amidst the pinecones. Consider using frosted ornaments and silver candleholders to tie in with your home's icy blue and silver colour scheme.

Cohesion, or a movement from room to room that connects everything, is the aim. Instead than feeling like a stand-alone production, your table should enhance the festive atmosphere in your house.

Let's now discuss the final elements, the little things that give this centrepiece its unique character. Not the kind of ribbons you use to wrap presents. Imagine silky, flowing ribbons that seem to belong among the foliage, perhaps made of velvet or satin. Knot them loosely so that the ends fall naturally over the table in a tasteful whisper of refinement.

The strong lines of the berries and pinecones are broken up by these ribbons, which give softness and movement. With each piece, you're including more layers, texture, and dimension.

Introduce a theme if you're feeling adventurous. Perhaps the focal point of your arrangement depicts a scene from a wintry woodland, complete with tiny creatures tucked into the foliage and sparkling lights. Alternatively, perhaps the theme is classic elegance, accentuated by antique ornaments and mercury glass candleholders.

Subtle decisions that establish a feeling of place and period are more important than a loud, overt subject. Even if it's just for a meal, your guests won't even notice the theme—instead, they'll simply experience the atmosphere you've created, which is like entering an other universe.

The finest aspect? To pull this off, you don't need a professional decorator or florist. This type of centerpiece's imperfection and ability to capture your style and home's essence are what make it so beautiful.

It's all about layering textures, bringing in warmth and invitingness with ribbons and candles, and adding depth. When you're through, your table will have taken on the role of the centre of your holiday gathering, where mouthwatering meals are shared and memories are created.

Creating a Candle and Pine Cone Display

I magine the setting: a table covered in the gentle light of a candle, pine cones strewn about like nature's glitter, and the scent of pine filling the air. The goal of this centrepiece is to capture the cosy, rustic charm of the holiday season rather than to be ostentatious. The most basic components are used first: pine cones and candles. A large impact may be created with little; it's all in the arrangement and the finishing touches that make the difference.

Assemble your supplies first. To fill in the spaces, gather a handful of pine cones, a few tall and short candles, and maybe some foliage. Consider the pine cones as the foundation of the natural world. They offer some texture and a hint of rustic elegance, so they're more than just decorations. Nothing elaborate needs to be done with them. Simply shake them briefly to remove any remaining pieces, then place them away. These basic cones are about to be transformed into something like to a wintry paradise.

Now concentrate on the candles. Select candles with different heights to add visual interest. The tallest candles should be positioned in the middle, with the shorter ones surrounding them. This design gains depth and attracts the eye with its staggered look. Use candles with delicate Christmas aromas, like cinnamon or pine, for a little more flair. Your table will become a sensory feast for all the senses as well as an eye feast thanks to the aroma, which will elevate the entire experience.

LET'S NOW EXPERIMENT a little bit with the positioning. Arrange a foundation of artificial or real foliage on your table. This will act as the background, bringing in a splash of green to accentuate the candles and pine cones. Arrange the pine cones in a cluster around the candles by arranging them amidst the foliage. Allow the cones to fall where they will, but maintain the tallest candles in the centre; you want the effect to be natural. In addition to creating a focal point, this enables the candles' light to elegantly reflect off the pine cones.

You might wish to give the pine cones a dusting of glitter or fake snow for a little festive charm. It resembles lightly dusting them with magic. Just don't go overboard. To capture that festive sparkle without overpowering the pine cones' natural beauty, only a slight touch is sufficient.

Remember to take the candle holders into account. To add a rustic touch, you could want to wrap some twine or ribbon over the glass holders you're using. Choose metallic candle holders that gleam and offer a touch of glitz for a more refined appearance.

Before placing the candles on the greenery, place them on these holders. The entire display is elevated by this little touch, which gives it a sophisticated yet approachable appearance.

Balance is the key to a beautiful show. Try arranging the candles and pine cones in different ways until you get the perfect arrangement. In addition to a variety of textures and heights, you want a sense of coherence. Consider the overall appearance instead of concentrating on each component separately.

Take frequent steps back to see how everything works together. There are situations when letting things fall into place organically results in the ideal arrangement.

Consider including a few tiny holiday-themed objects in your centrepiece if you want to give it a little more flair. Add a little additional holiday charm with little ornaments, tiny present boxes, or even a few sprigs of holly. Distribute these tiny objects amid the candles and pine cones, making sure they enhance rather than clash with the focal points of your arrangement.

Adding Snow and Sparkle for the Finishing Touch

Imagine this: with a few simple adjustments, your table, which is already decorated with pine cones and candles, transforms into a stunning winter paradise. Not merely decorations, faux snow and well-placed lighting are the secret sauce that elevates an ordinary centrepiece into a spectacular work of art.

First, the fake snow. It's more about incorporating a little bit of that wintry flair than making your table look like a snowstorm.

Dust the base of the candle and pine cone arrangement with a small dusting of snow. The snow should sparkle and catch the light, giving the entire scene a clean, frosty appearance. It appears as though a light snowfall has kissed your table, bringing the classic winter charm into your house.

Select artificial snow by selecting varieties with a hint of gloss or sparkle. The goal here is to capture the light in a way that feels mystical, not to create a snowstorm. Lightly scatter it between the pine cones and around the base of the candles.

A little goes a long way; if you use too much, you run the risk of overpowering your centerpiece's inherent beauty. Instead of concealing the components you've already assembled, aim for a light dusting that brings them to life.

Consider lighting next. Setting the right tone is important, but so is ensuring that your focal point is the star of the show. Little LED lights are ideal for this kind of work. They offer a gentle, ambient glow and are simple to incorporate into your arrangement without taking centre stage.

Make sure to evenly arrange them for a pleasing look by wrapping them around your candles or tucking them in among the pine cones. The goal is to generate a soft illumination that highlights the imitation snow's brilliance and gives your holiday table a cosy warmth.

Consider adding a little fairy dust, figuratively speaking, if you're feeling really daring. Little sequins or glitter can be used as shimmering touches to provide a magical touch to the snow by catching the light. Remember that nuance is essential.

Instead of competing with the rest of your centrepiece, you want these accents to accentuate it. Your table will look extra shimmery without coming across as garish with a little touch.

Consider where you want your centrepiece to be as well. The ideal location is one that is both safe from probable mishaps and allows for admiration. Make sure that nothing that could catch fire is too close to the real candles, if you're using them. First and foremost, safety! Place your centrepiece where it will be nicely accentuated by the lights and where it won't be knocked over or jostled during your vacation meals.

Examine the environment surrounding your table. If there is overhead lighting in your dining room, turn it down a little so that the candles and fairy lights shine. As you prepare a buffet or a more relaxed dining setting, make sure the space is well-lit, with the focal point being your centrepiece. The goal is to create a spectacular focal point that captures attention and establishes the mood for your joyous occasion.

REMEMBER TO KEEP IT private as well. Your centrepiece ought to convey your own festive vibe. Add a few little, sentimental items, such as tiny ornaments or mementos with Christmas themes that hold particular significance for you. Your centrepiece becomes a part of your holiday tale rather than merely a decoration thanks to these little touches.

CHAPTER 4
OUTDOOR LIGHT DISPLAYS

Nothing quite like an exterior light show to turn your house into a winter paradise during the holiday season. Imagine your home decked out with sparkling lights that provide a mesmerising show against the night sky and entice onlookers to stop and enjoy the holiday spirit. It takes more than just stringing up a few lights to transform your house into a magical holiday light display at night.

To begin, make sure your home is well-lit throughout. Making a frame that draws attention to the building is the aim. To draw attention to the doors, windows, and roofline, use lighting. LED strands are great for this work; they're bright, energy-efficient, and can cover a lot of ground without depleting your pocketbook. Make sure the lights are placed equally as you drape them to prevent any uneven areas. A house that appears to glitter from every perspective, with one area of lights flowing smoothly into the next, has a very appealing quality.

Next, think about giving your display more depth and dimension. Here, ground lights might be very helpful. Arrange them in flower beds, roads, and sidewalks. These lights offer a layer of brilliance that dances beneath guests' feet in addition as directing them to your entrance. If you have any shrubs or trees in your yard, consider stringing lights around them to frame your house with blazing columns of colour. It's similar to dotting your landscape with stars; each one enhances the overall picture.

Do not be afraid to use figures and inflatables for a whimsical touch. You can use snowmen, Santa, and reindeer as whimsical centre pieces for your presentation. Arrange them in a festive manner to greet guests, maybe in your front garden or next to your entry. Just watch the size; although smaller decorations could get lost, larger ones might quickly overtake your room. To make sure these components work in harmony with your lights rather than against them, balance is essential.

RECALL THAT IT'S NOT just about the lighting. Think about using wreaths and lit garlands in your design. An attractive and cosy entrance is created by a lit wreath on the front door. Likewise, draping a garland over a window frame or encircling a railing gives your display a sense of refinement and coherence. Select garlands with integrated lights for a seamless appearance that doesn't involve any extra wiring or trouble.

INCLUDE A FEW PROJECTORS or color-changing lights in your setup to improve the atmosphere. Color-changing lights give your display a dynamic touch by cycling through different hues and bringing life to your garden. On the other hand, projectors can add an extra layer of enchantment to your home's front without requiring a complex setup by casting Christmas sceneries or snowflake patterns across it.

Priority one when installing outdoor lighting is safety. Make sure you're utilising extension cords rated for outdoor use and that all electrical connections are tight. Stakes in the ground can assist keep cords tight and avoid trip hazards. If you use timers, be sure they are programmed to switch the lights on and off at the proper times so you don't leave them on all night. It's a simple action that can conserve energy and avert possible problems.

Your lighting setup has a big influence on the final result. Choose simple, geometric patterns and minimalist motifs for a more contemporary appearance.

Choosing the Right Lights and Placement

The appropriate lights, in the correct places, may truly transform your house into a festive wonderland. With so many variations available, selecting outdoor-rated string lights can seem like a difficult endeavour. Prioritise quality and safety first. Make sure the lights you choose are marked for outdoor usage; this ensures that they are weatherproof and lowers the possibility of electrical problems. Here, LED lights are a great option because they're long-lasting, energy-efficient, and, best of all, they remain cool to the touch—a benefit if you want to use them near combustible materials.

Think about the kind of light you intend to utilise. While coloured lights lend an obvious holiday flair, clear lights have a timeless, elegant appearance. You may choose lights with various effects, like chasing or twinkling, for a little entertainment value. These can be combined to provide a visually striking, dynamic display that glows in the dark.

THE LENGTH OF THE STRING lights should be chosen based on the size of the area and the desired level of coverage. The secret is to choose lights that complement your overall eyesight and are adaptable enough to function in various environments.

It's placement that makes the difference. Determine which locations will have the greatest influence when you first lay out your space. Draw the outline of your rooftop for a striking appearance.

THIS TIMELESS METHOD draws attention to your home's architectural details and produces a powerful silhouette. Put lights on fences, railings, and columns to bring the holiday spirit inside. Observe how the lights fall; any inconsistencies or holes can take away from the overall effect.

Don't overlook the power supply. Make sure the outlets and extension cords you have outside are suitable for the task. To avoid electrical accidents, look for extension cords that are waterproof and use GFCI outlets.

Use an outside power strip (avoid overloading it) if you need to connect more than one string of lights. A significant aspect of the Christmas spirit is safety.

Consider layering if you want your lighting design to stand out. Using a variety of lighting fixtures together can provide depth and interest. Spotlights highlighting your landscaping, for example, would go well with the string lights on the house. Alternatively, combine big, vibrant bulbs with fairy lights to produce a whimsical contrast.

Adding layers to your display can give it texture and make it stand out even from a distance.

The impact of your lights is also affected by the height at which you hang them. Higher-hung lights can illuminate a larger space and produce a dramatic display, while lower-hung lights highlight particular details. When dealing with trees, use lights to create a cascading effect by wrapping them around the trunk and branches and leaving some hanging loose. This technique gives your garden a charming, natural appearance.

Before deciding on the ultimate location for your lights, give them some testing time. Once plugged in, make any necessary adjustments. This stage makes sure everything is functioning properly and lets you view how they appear in various settings. Once the necessary modifications have been made, fasten the lights firmly using outdoor-grade clips or hooks. This keeps your lights exactly where you want them and helps avoid sagging.

USING SMART PLUGS OR light timers to automate your display is another piece of advice. Timers allow you to set precise times for turning on and off your lights, which saves energy in addition to being convenient. With the use of voice assistants or smartphones, you can manage your lights more conveniently with smart plugs. With this extra convenience, you may effortlessly change your display from the comforts of your own home.

FOR A FINISHED LOOK, add lighting to your landscaping. Use string lights or ground lights to draw attention to shrubs, garden beds, and paths. With this method, the transition from your house to your garden is smoothed out, giving the whole space a joyful, welcoming vibe. For an additional whimsical touch that goes well with your main display, you may also think about adding garden stakes or illuminated ornaments.

Enhancing with Garlands and LED Shapes

I magine your house covered in lights, with LED shapes bringing a touch of magic to the night and garlands hung like glistening ribbons. LED forms and glowing garlands can take your outdoor display from appealing to spectacular. With these additions, your yard may become a fanciful wonderland where every piece contributes to a spectacular Christmas show.

BEGIN WITH GARLANDS. You may hang these adaptable decorations over fences, railings, and entrances. They are made of a variety of materials, such as burlap, tinsel, and greenery. Whether it's a traditional evergreen garland or something more contemporary, pick a garland that goes well with your current décor. Choose garlands that have LED lights integrated into them for extra glitz. Rich textures and gentle lighting work together to create a cosy, welcoming ambiance.

WHEN HANGING GARLANDS, follow your imagination. You can hang them from the ceiling of a covered porch, wrap them over the rails of your staircase, or drape them over your front door. Every location presents a fresh chance to elevate the joyous atmosphere. Use outdoor-rated garland hooks or clips to keep everything organised. This keeps the garlands from drooping or sagging and keeps their polished appearance.

LET'S NOW DISCUSS LED shapes. These aren't your typical Christmas lights. Imagine candy canes that glow, snowflakes that shimmer, and stars that twinkle to bring some fun to your display. LED shapes are available in a variety of designs, each bringing a unique touch of magic. Arrange them in strategic locations throughout your garden to generate eye-catching focal points. You could string stars from the eaves, plant a snowflake in a tree or line a walkway with glistening candy canes.

WHEN WORKING WITH LED forms, consider layering. To add depth and intrigue, pair them with garlands and string lights. For example, adorn a tree trunk with a garland and place LED snowflakes on it. Alternatively, hang a string of lights over a fence and space out the bright stars to anchor the strand. This kind of layering improves the aesthetic appeal and gives the design a dynamic, dynamic feel.

THINK ABOUT HOW BIG your LED shapes are. While smaller decorations can be dotted throughout for a more understated look, larger ones can serve as statement pieces. Try a variety of sizes and locations to determine what suits your area the best. Don't be afraid to mix and combine forms to offer variety and surprise.

For a touch of refinement, combine your LED forms with the color scheme of your garlands. If your garland is classic green, gold LED forms might give a classy touch.

For a futuristic twist, mix silver garlands with cool blue LED forms. Matching colors enhances the harmony of your presentation and ensures a unified effect.

Safety is always a priority, especially with outside decorations. Make sure all LED forms and garlands are suitable for outdoor use to endure the weather conditions. In order to avoid any risks, periodically inspect the wiring and connections. Make sure everything is securely fastened to prevent mishaps or harm.

CHAPTER 5
DIY GIFT WRAPPING

Present-opening is always exciting, but there's also excitement in gift-wrapping. Not only should the present be hidden, but your wrapping should also make a statement and elevate each gift to the status of a work of art. Here's how to elevate the simple act of gift wrapping so that your presents become the talk of the Christmas get-together.

STARTING WITH THE ESSENTIALS, pick a wrapping paper that complements the current season. Though classic motifs like candy canes, snowflakes, and reindeer are always popular, don't be scared to try out unique prints or even homemade creations. Consider using kraft paper and making your own decorations to add a personalised touch. It's a blank canvas waiting for your imagination to go wild.

After choosing your paper, you need to consider the wrapping method. While precision is important, perfection is not necessary.

A neat, clean fold can make all the difference. To make sure the gift is entirely covered, measure out enough paper to cover it completely, plus a little overlap. To maintain neat and concealed seams, use double-sided tape and a sharp pair of scissors for precise cutting.

Let's now go to the enjoyable portion: the embellishments. Here, tags, bows, and ribbons are your pals. A plain parcel can be made into something amazing with ribbons. Choose twine for a rustic appearance or large satin ribbons for an opulent effect.

Experiment with different textures and colors to find what complements your paper and enhances the overall effect.

Another great method to add flair is with bows. Although pre-made bows are available, making your own has a unique quality. Using a small amount of tape or glue, secure the ribbon bow to the top of the gift. What was the outcome? a polished gift that appears to have been purchased from a boutique.

REMEMBER TO INCLUDE gift tags. They offer a chance to add a whimsical touch or a personal message in addition to being utilitarian. With some imagination and cardstock, make your own tags. Write a sincere remark or decorate with stickers and stamps. For a more finished appearance, tie a piece of string or ribbon around the tag.

If you want to add even more inventiveness, think about using natural materials. You may tie little ornaments, holly leaves, or pinecones onto the ribbon to give it an extra festive feel.

Just be sure that any extra components are firmly fastened to prevent loss or damage.

Stacked wrapping is an additional creative idea. After wrapping the gift in one kind of paper, around the centre with a belt of contrasting paper. Using this approach, your wrapping will have more depth and appeal. To bring everything together, tie a bow or ribbon in contrasting colours. It's an easy trick with a powerful effect.

KEEP YOUR WRAPPING space tidy at all times. Your ability to concentrate on the details and enjoy the process will both benefit from a clutter-free desk. As you work on each gift, take your time and keep all of your supplies close at hand. You can use wrapping to showcase your artistic side and add a personal touch to every gift.

If someone enjoys a challenge, think of wrapping presents in unusual ways. Wrap your gifts with antique maps, cloth squares, or scarves.

THESE UNUSUAL MATERIALS can give the gift-giving experience a personalised touch and increase its memorability.

Use secret messaging or concealed chambers to add aspects of surprise. For instance, tuck a smaller gift or a letter into a bigger box. It increases the recipient's level of enthusiasm and makes the unwrapping experience more interesting.

Designing Custom Gift Tags Using Ornaments

Personalised gift tags created from handcrafted decorations make every gift a joyful surprise. It takes more than just tying a name tag on a gift; it takes putting your own unique flair and originality into each one. This is how to turn those treasured homemade ornaments into unique gift tags that will really make your gifts pop.

Assemble your ornaments first. Consider the ones you've produced over the years; whether they have a small crack, an unusual shape, or they just didn't quite match the motif of your tree, but they are too valuable to throw away. These are ideal candidates for the gift tag position you have taken on.

First, get the decorations ready. If they are excessively large, think about pruning them to a more manageable size. You may trim off any extra pieces with a pair of wire cutters, leaving you with a piece that is the ideal size for a tag. Next, to provide a smooth surface for writing or decorating, give them a moderate sanding if they have a shiny finish or sharp edges.

It's now time to transform these ornaments into useful gift tags. Tie a tiny length of ribbon or string around each ornament. This will serve as your attachment point, so pick something attractive and robust. If the ornament doesn't already have a tiny hole in the top, create one with a drill or needle and thread the string through it. Make a tight knot, leaving a small amount of string hanging for simple gift attachment.

Let's start experimenting with the design now. One way to get started is to customise each ornament.

Write the recipient's name or a brief, heartfelt note right on the ornament using paint or a fine-tipped marker. Make sure the paint is totally dry before handling it if you're using it to prevent smudging. Add little drawings of stars, hearts, or snowflakes to the name to give it a festive feel.

Add some glitter or embellishments to add a little more pzazz. A little glitter glue can transform an ordinary ornament into something dazzling and joyous. As an alternative, add tiny stones or stickers for a texture and colour burst.

Just make sure that whatever you add is firmly fastened and won't come loose while being handled.

Think about layering for a more put together appearance. A tiny piece of patterned fabric or paper should be wrapped around the ornament before it is fastened to the present. This can give your gift presentation more depth and make a lovely contrast with the ornament. To make sure the paper or fabric stays in place, use a hot glue gun to attach it.

Crafting Elegant Wrapping Paper with Stencils and Paint

Making your own wrapping paper is a creative way to add a festive and unique touch to your gifts. Why not put on some elbow grease and create something truly original rather than settle for designs that you can buy at the store? Here's how you use paints, stencils, and stamps to create unique wrapping paper.

Prioritise your supplies by gathering them first. A roll of plain wrapping paper, which serves as your canvas, is required.

Select a smooth, high-quality paper for optimal outcomes. Additionally, you'll need stencils or stamps featuring festive designs, like holly, stars, or snowflakes. Next are paints, which have festive hues like gold, silver, scarlet, and green. Use cardboard or foam sheets to create your own if you don't have any stencils or stamps.

Set up your workplace first. To prevent paint spatters from landing on your surfaces, spread out a sizable piece of plastic or old newspapers. Because paints can be extremely powerful, make sure your workspace has adequate ventilation. To keep your plain wrapping paper flat, roll it out and tape the edges.

Let's talk about stencils now. Should you be utilising pre-made stencils, affix them to the paper using painter's tape to avoid any movement. Paint over the stencil using a brush or sponge. Avoid loading your brush with too much paint as this might cause the design to become hazy and seep under the stencil. Dabbing the paint on will result in a clear, sharp image. When you've finished covering the stencil area, carefully pull it off, allowing the paper to dry before continuing to a new portion or stencil application.

A fun substitute is to make your own stencils if you're handy with do-it-yourself projects. Cut foam sheets or cardboard into Christmas shapes. Make sure the shapes are big enough so the wrapping paper has a recognisable design on it. When your stencils are prepared, proceed as before: attach the stencil, apply a little paint, and carefully pull it off. There are countless creative and customisable options with this approach.

ANOTHER FANTASTIC TOOL for creating wrapping paper designs is a stamp. You can use stamps you buy at the market or carve potatoes or foam to make your own. Press down firmly on the wrapping paper after dipping your stamp into the paint. To establish a recurring pattern, repeat as necessary. Try a variety of colours and stamp positions until you find a layout that you adore. As with stencils, wait until the paint is completely dry before proceeding.

YOUR WRAPPING PAPER gains depth and interest when you layer designs. Begin by applying a foundation colour and allow it to fully dry. Next, apply a contrasting design on top using stencils or stamps. Using this method, you may produce a gorgeous, multi-dimensional effect that improves the wrapping paper's overall appearance.

Remember to include your unique touches. You might write names or other text directly onto the wrapping paper using a little brush. For an added sparkle, think about including little elements like glitter or metallic accents.

CHAPTER 6
THE GRAND FINALE

The culmination of your holiday makeover is the moment when everything comes together to generate an amazing Christmas fantasy. At this point, everything matters, and magic actually happens. This is your time to make your vision of the holidays come to life, from the cheery decorations that greet your guests to the sparkling lights that dance around your house.

Start with your exterior exhibit; see it as the main doorway leading into your winter wonderland. Your home should be a warm, welcoming haven. Start by draping strings of sparkling lights over the windows and down the eaves to create an outline for your house. Whether it's a striking multicoloured scheme, a traditional white scheme, or a combination of the two, pick a colour scheme that works with your overall concept. Remember to add some larger, eye-catching components to create a whimsical vibe, such as lit snowmen or reindeer.

Glam up the scene with festive garlands and wreaths as you move to the front yard or porch. Garlands can be wrapped over front door edges, posts, and railings. Make them stand out by adding some ribbons and sparkling lights. Create a wreath that is both sophisticated and endearing by combining conventional greenery with seasonal trinkets. A beautifully decorated front entrance gives off an appealing vibe and lets visitors know they are about to enter a magnificent place.

Let the magic continue inside your house with a beautifully decorated Christmas tree. Choose a position where the tree may be admired from many angles. Adorn it with a combination of traditional and unique decorations. Light strings ought to wind their way between the trees, leaving plenty room for ornaments, tinsel, and garlands. Add a tree topper that ties in with your overall motif, such as an angel, star, or something special that you own.

ANOTHER MAIN FEATURE is your dining room. Use serviette rings, place settings and seasonal centrepieces to turn your table into a feast fit for a king or queen. The scene can be set with a table runner in vibrant, festive colours. Think about combining natural materials, such as holly and pinecones, with tiny, dazzling ornaments or candles. Every setting should have a unique atmosphere with well-considered accents that make every visitor feel honoured.

THE AMBIENT DECORATIONS serve as the final detail. Christmas stockings should be carefully hung, with unique accents that capture the essence of each family member. Your living areas will seem cosier and more festive if you scatter festive blankets and pillows throughout them. Use diffusers or candles to add Christmas fragrances, making the smell experience complement the visual extravaganza.

YOUR HOUSE MIGHT HAVE a wonderland feel in every area. Place garlands or artwork with holiday themes next to picture frames and mantels as little finishing touches. Arrange festive figurines or vignettes in unexpected places, such as a festive scene atop a bookshelf or a tray filled with Christmas delicacies on the coffee table.

Play some of your favourite holiday songs on a playlist; music makes the atmosphere better. The right music elevates the experience and fills the house with a happy vibe that spreads throughout.

Coordinating Indoor and Outdoor Decorations

Imagine coming into a warm and inviting space that feels like a natural continuation of your outdoor holiday display after stepping out into the crisp winter air. When you create a cohesive flow between your outside and internal decorations, your house becomes a fully furnished winter paradise, with each area complementing the others.

TO BEGIN WITH, CHOOSE a colour scheme that works in both spaces. Select hues that complement indoor spaces nicely and perform well in natural daylight. A cohesive look can be achieved using traditional red and green, icy blue and silver, or sophisticated gold and white. Every change from the exterior to the inside feels planned and purposeful when your colours coordinate.

Consider your front yard to be a magnificent introduction from the outside. Guests are led to your door by a gorgeously lit pathway, through which the first glimpses of your indoor theme appear. As guests enter your home, use complementing lights or garlands on your outdoor railings to direct their gaze with the same colours and patterns.

Visitors should sense the same wonder they did outside as soon as they enter. Take care of your entryway first. Decorate it in a way that reflects your outside theme. If you used icicles and snowflakes outdoors, carry over that theme inside with a glittering garland or a snowy wreath.

THIS ESTABLISHES AN instantaneous link between the two areas and prepares the viewer for a seamless encounter.

Bring this harmony indoors with your tree décor. If you have decorated your outdoor space with bright, huge lights, consider using somewhat smaller, comparable lights for your Christmas tree. Continue using decorations and ornaments that go with your outdoor theme. You could even use some of the same colour or pattern from your tree decorations.

ANOTHER CRUCIAL PLACE where this synchronisation excels is the dining area. If your dining area has exterior lights that twinkle, replicate the effect inside with candlelight or string lights around the sides. A table centrepiece that complements your outdoor decor's hues and design elements unifies the entire look.

Consider layering when it comes to decorations. For instance, incorporate rustic charm items such as hessian and pinecones into your inside decor if your outside space has a similar concept.

Similarly, for whimsical themes, bring the enjoyment outdoors with colourful decorations and festive designs.

Remember the specifics. Complement the indoor and outdoor garlands and wreaths. Look for interior lights that have the same colour as your outdoor lights, if they are warm white. This kind of meticulous attention to detail keeps the overall design of your house consistent.

THE SMOOTH BLEND IS enhanced by even the smallest details. Use identical bows or ribbons indoors and outdoors. Choose a complementary piece for the interior if you have a certain ornament or decoration outside. There is a sense of intentionality and oneness created by these tiny echoes.

Additionally, interactive components like homemade crafts or customised decorations help close the gap. If you make personalised tree ornaments, think about creating matching products for outdoor exhibits, or the other way around.

Adding Scent and Sound for a Multi-Sensory Holiday Atmosphere

Imagine being greeted by a cosy, joyous embrace that satisfies every sensation as soon as you enter your house during the holidays. It's more important to consider how something makes you feel than how it looks. In order to transform your house into an authentic holiday paradise, you must create a multi-auditory experience that embodies the spirit of Christmas throughout the entire space.

BEGIN WITH FRAGRANCE. It's amazing how quickly memories and emotions associated with holidays may be evoked by a well-known scent. Classic Christmas scents like pine, cinnamon, and nutmeg take you to crowded festive markets and icy woodlands. Fill your home with the traditional holiday scent by simmering cinnamon sticks on the stove or lighting candles scented with pine. You can utilise essential oil diffusers for a more understated look. Select mixes that have a hint of citrus mixed with pine to create a clean, energising ambiance. Recall that the goal is to leave the room with a hint of aroma without overpowering it.

Then think about how music makes the holidays more festive. The proper songs may turn your house into a festive refuge since music has the ability to instantly create the tone. Make a playlist with your all-time favourite Christmas songs, from lively seasonal tunes to classic carols. Organise your speakers so that the music flows across the room rather than just booming from one spot. Make playlists appropriate for various times of the day.

Traditional carols mixed in a gentle way can greet guests, while more upbeat, contemporary music might liven up your Christmas gatherings.

Don't limit yourself to music, though. Consider including soundscapes that enhance the festive mood. Think of ambient sounds, such as the soft patter of falling snow or the crackling of a fire. These options are available on a lot of sound devices and apps, which further enhances the immersion. To add a whimsical element, you might even wish to have a few festive bells or chimes that sound as visitors enter particular rooms.

Another component of this multisensory experience is texture. Cosy rugs, fluffy pillows, and soft throws entice visitors to unwind and embrace the festive atmosphere. Select textures that warm up the room and go well with your décor. Knitted textiles, velvet, and faux fur all convey cosiness and celebration. Place these things in the living room or reading nook, or any other area where people congregate organically.

DESPITE THEIR IMPORTANCE, visual components function best when paired with sound and smell. The beauty of festive displays, the shimmer of decorations, and the brightness of glittering lights all add to the entire experience. Make sure all of these visual accents are visible from different areas of your house so that the visual feast is continuous. The play of light and shadow heightens the festive mood by providing depth and intrigue.

CONSIDER INCORPORATING these sensory aspects into your holiday customs for an extra special touch. Establish a family tradition that includes lighting a special candle, listening to your favourite Christmas music, and sipping hot beverages. These times turn into treasured customs that heighten the enchantment of the season and create a cosy, happy atmosphere in your house.

SUMMARY

Let's finish this voyage together by turning your house into a vacation haven. Imagine this: the sight, sound, and aroma of your home are all perfectly blended together to create a dazzling beacon of holiday pleasure. A mystical winter wonderland-like mood is created by the attention to every last detail and corner.

Begin by imagining your room transformed into a warm and welcoming retreat over the holidays. The aroma of freshly made cookies, cinnamon, and pine greets you warmly as soon as you walk in. This is about creating a sensory experience that welcomes everyone who goes through your door, not just putting up a few decorations.

Consider the holiday lights as something more than just decorative lighting. They are the stars of your outdoor display, illuminating your house like a beacon of joy. Select light strings that go with your style; go for a bold colour scheme for a lively, entertaining display, or a classic white for an exquisite appearance.

ARRANGE THEM IN A WAY that best showcases your home's architectural elements, and don't forget to encircle trees and bushes with them for an extra magical touch.

Once inside, your décor can showcase your artistic side over the holidays. Imagine a large centrepiece for your dining room table, a composition of pine cones and candles that combines the beauty of nature with a touch of holiday magic. Add some fake snow around it and soft lighting to enhance its allure. Every meal will feel like a special occasion thanks to this straightforward yet effective mix that produces a visual focus point.

Use your creativity when it comes to packaging presents. Make your own wrapping paper using festive paints and stencils. Each gift is made distinctive by this personal touch, which also increases the recipient's delight. Use handcrafted decorations as gift tags to add a personalised, handcrafted touch to gifts.

Use this same inventiveness to your outdoor décor, where LED forms and garlands add whimsy and appeal to your setup.

Let the patterns that resemble snowflakes, stars, or even playful creatures adorn your front yard. This creates a sense of awe that will enthral both onlookers and your guests.

Make sure your exterior and inside decorations are coordinated for a fully festive feel to your property. Ensure that your internal themes flow naturally to the outside, producing a coherent design that binds the entire home together. This unity between interior and outside décor intensifies the magical effect and makes your home a standout during the festive season.

Of course, don't discount the influence of sound and smell as well. Bring in holiday scents like cinnamon and pine to create the perfect atmosphere for the holidays. To set the mood, pair this with a carefully chosen playlist of beloved Christmas songs. With this multi-sensory approach, you can be sure that every time someone visits your house, they are immersed in a festive atmosphere.

STRATEGIC ACTION PLAN

1. Planning and Budgeting

- **Set Goals:** Determine the overall vision for your holiday décor. Decide if you want a classic, modern, or whimsical look.

- **Create a Budget:** Outline how much you're willing to spend on decorations, lights, and other elements. Allocate funds to different categories, such as outdoor lights, indoor decorations, and gift-wrapping materials.

2. Designing the Layout

- **Indoor Décor:** Sketch a basic layout of where you want to place major decorations. Consider focal points like the living room, dining area, and entryway.

- **Outdoor Décor:** Plan the placement of lights, garlands, and other outdoor elements. Identify key areas such as the front yard, porch, and windows.

3. SHOPPING AND ACQUIRING Supplies

- **Compile a List:** Make a list of all the items you need, including lights, ornaments, wrapping paper, stencils, and other supplies.

- **Purchase Items:** Buy your decorations, ensuring you get high-quality, safe materials. Look for sales or discounts to stay within budget.

4. Execution of Décor Installation

- **Outdoor Lights:** Begin by installing outdoor lights. Test them before mounting to ensure they work properly. Use extension cords and timers as needed for convenience.

- **Indoor Decorations:** Start with larger items like the tree and major centerpieces. Then add smaller decorations such as candles, pine cones, and garlands.

- **Gift Wrapping:** Craft your custom wrapping paper and tags. Set up a wrapping station to streamline the process and ensure consistency.

5. Adding Final Touches

- **Scent and Sound:** Place scented candles or diffusers throughout your home. Create a playlist of holiday music to play in the background, enhancing the festive atmosphere.

- **Check Cohesion:** Ensure that your indoor and outdoor décor harmonize. Make adjustments as needed to maintain a cohesive look.

6. Maintenance and Updates

- **Regular Checks:** Periodically check lights and decorations to ensure everything is functioning properly.

- **Refresh Décor:** Update or replace any items that may have become damaged or outdated. Keep an eye out for new decorations that may enhance your theme.

7. Gathering Feedback

- **Ask for Opinions:** Get feedback from family and friends about your décor. Use their insights to make any final tweaks.

- **Evaluate Impact:** Reflect on what worked well and what could be improved for future holiday seasons.

8. Enjoy the Season

- **Host Events:** Invite friends and family over to enjoy your transformed space. Plan festive activities like holiday parties, dinners, or movie nights.

- **Celebrate:** Take time to appreciate your hard work and enjoy the magical atmosphere you've created.

By following this strategic action plan, you can ensure that your home is transformed into a festive wonderland that captivates and delights everyone who visits.

Don't miss out!

Visit the website below and you can sign up to receive emails whenever NORA GREY publishes a new book. There's no charge and no obligation.

https://books2read.com/r/B-A-DJAKC-GHDAF

BOOKS 2 READ

Connecting independent readers to independent writers.

Did you love *How to Transform Your Home into a Christmas Wonderland : Turn Your Home into Santa's Magical Wonderland*? Then you should read *How to Celebrate a Debt-Free Christmas : Jingle All the Way to a Debt-Free Christmas!*[1] by NORA GREY!

[2]

The holiday season sparkles with joy and warmth, yet lurking beneath the twinkling lights and festive gatherings is a darker reality—a financial storm that sweeps through the United States every year. According to recent statistics, an overwhelming number of Americans find themselves drowning in debt as they struggle to meet the demands of the holiday season. The numbers tell a tale of stress and financial strain, with countless families falling into the trap of overspending, only to face the harsh consequences when the holiday cheer fades away.

Statistics paint a grim picture: nearly 60% of Americans admit to incurring debt during the holiday season, with the average amount hovering around $1,000. This debt isn't just a temporary setback; it often lingers well into the new

1. https://books2read.com/u/bayNn6

2. https://books2read.com/u/bayNn6

year, creating a cycle of financial stress that overshadows the joy of the season. The impact is felt across all demographics, with young families, in particular, feeling the pinch as they try to balance holiday cheer with financial responsibility.

But what if there was a way to break free from this cycle? A way to enjoy the magic of the holidays without sacrificing your financial well-being? The answer lies in a simple yet powerful strategy: planning, discipline, and a mindset shift. By taking control of your finances before the holiday season begins, you can avoid the pitfalls that so many Americans fall into year after year.

The holiday season doesn't have to be a time of financial recklessness. Instead, it can be a time of joy and generosity, free from the chains of debt. The key is to start early, setting clear financial goals and sticking to them. This means creating a budget that reflects your true financial situation, not just your holiday wishes. It's about making thoughtful choices, whether that means scaling back on expensive gifts, opting for homemade or heartfelt presents, or finding creative ways to celebrate without breaking the bank.

Recent statistics reveal that 28% of Americans enter the new year with more debt than they had at the start of the holiday season. This burden isn't just financial; it takes a toll on mental and emotional health as well.

Consider this: the true spirit of the holidays isn't found in extravagant gifts or lavish parties. It's in the moments of connection with loved ones, the warmth of shared experiences, and the simple joys that don't come with a price tag. By focusing on these aspects of the season, you can create lasting memories that aren't tied to financial strain.

The statistics are clear: 1 in 5 Americans will take over three months to pay off their holiday debt, with many taking much longer. This prolonged financial burden can turn the joy of the holiday season into a source of dread. But by making smart financial choices, you can avoid this fate and start the new year with a sense of financial security and peace of mind.

The holiday season is a time for giving, but it's also a time for taking care of yourself and your financial future. By setting boundaries, being mindful of your spending, and making thoughtful choices, you can enjoy all the magic of the season without the financial hangover that so many Americans experience.

Recent data shows that over 50% of Americans regret their holiday spending once the season is over. This regret isn't just about the money—it's about the missed opportunities to celebrate in a way that aligns with your values and financial goals. By taking a proactive approach to your holiday finances, you can avoid this regret and focus on what truly matters: the joy of the season and the people you share it with.

Start planning now, set clear financial goals, and embrace the true spirit of the holidays—one that celebrates the things that really matter.

Also by NORA GREY

Health Beyond Christmas : How to Stay Healthy and Savor the Season of
Christmas with Joy, Not Regret
How to Celebrate a Debt-Free Christmas : Jingle All the Way to a Debt-Free
Christmas!
The Spanish Art of Christmas Gift Boxing : Elevate Your Gift-Giving Game
with Exquisite Spanish Boxing Techniques
How to Celebrate Christmas With a Flat Belly : The Ultimate Flat Belly
Christmas Guide
The Pre-Christmas & Post-Christmas Bliss : Your Ultimate Guide to a Magical
Christmas Season and Beyond
Christmas in Paris : How to Celebrate Christmas Like a Local in Paris
Christmas in Spain : How to Celebrate Christmas the Spanish Way
Christmas Shopping in Barcelona : Where to Shop in Barcelona Like a Local
How to Transform Your Home into a Christmas Wonderland : Turn Your
Home into Santa's Magical Wonderland